Kobe's Quest

ILLUSTRATED BY
Adrian Hayles

DEVELOPED BY
Alexis Dawson

WRITTEN BY
Natasha Henry-Dixon

A Crabtree Forest Book

Crabtree Publishing
crabtreebooks.com

Written by: Natasha Henry-Dixon
Illustrated by: Adrian Hayles
Developed by: Alexis Dawson
Editors: Janine Deschenes, Ellen Rodger, Melissa Boyce
Proofreader: Kathy Middleton
Designed by: Tammy McGarr
Production manager: Candice Campbell

Crabtree Publishing

crabtreebooks.com 800-387-7650

 In Canada: We acknowledge the financial support of the Government of Canada through the Canada Book Fund for our publishing activities.

Printed in the U.S.A./CP2025

Published in Canada
Crabtree Publishing
616 Welland Ave.
St. Catharines, Ontario
L2M 5V6

Published in the United States
Crabtree Publishing
347 Fifth Ave
Suite 1402-145
New York, NY 10016

Library and Archives Canada Cataloguing in Publication
Available at Library and Archives Canada

Library of Congress Cataloging-in-Publication Data
Available at the Library of Congress

Hardcover: 978-1-0398-8127-3
Paperback: 978-1-0398-8488-5
Ebook (pdf): 978-1-0398-8247-8
Epub: 978-1-0398-8367-3

Table of Contents

Hi! I'm Kobe. I am 12 years old. I live with my mom, dad, and sister. My parents are from Ghana, a country in West Africa with people from many cultures and backgrounds. I have been there twice to visit my grandparents, aunts, uncles, and cousins. I love playing video games with my cousins, and soccer, which my father calls football.
KOBE
Hey, I'm Jordyn and I'm 12. I live with my auntie. She says I'm "introspective," which I guess means I like to think a lot. And I do! I also like to act on my thoughts and beliefs. I love libraries because they are places where I can explore everything. I also love my cat, Thelonious, who always gets into good trouble.

Assalamu alaikum! In Arabic, Aleemah means wise, or learned. I was named after my grandmother. I am 12 years old and I live with my parents, grandparents, two brothers, and one sister. We were all born in Sudan, a country in northeast Africa. I speak three languages and love to read, eat, and listen to my haboba's stories. That's my grandmother.
I'm De'Rico. I'm 13 and live with my mom and two sisters. My nani lives two streets over, which is great because I get to go over a lot and eat her delicious food anytime I want. I love to joke around and have fun with my friends. My favorite subject in school is science because I really love to figure things out.

IN A PARK NEAR YOU...
Hey, Kobe! Kobe!
That's my name. Don't wear it out!
Ha ha, very funny, Kobe. What does your name mean, anyway? I always wanted to ask you.
My parents wanted me to have an African name, because...
Hi Kobe, hi De'Rico. What are you up to?

We were just talking. Kobe was telling me about his name.
What does your name mean, Kobe?
My parents told me my name means "born on Tuesday." They chose it to connect me to my Ghanaian heritage.
I like that. Wouldn't it be cool to travel to West Africa to learn more about where your family came from?
We could learn about your ancestors. Yeah! Let's travel back to your roots.

KOBE

HOMELAND AFRICA

The first human **ancestors**, called hominids, came from Africa. Some of the earliest fossils of these ancestors have been found in East and Southern Africa. These early humans migrated throughout Africa, and later into Europe and Asia around 1.8 million years ago.

This world map shows the Gall-Peters **projection**. It is an equal-area projection, which means that it shows the true size of a place. The Gall-Peters projection more accurately represents the size of Africa.

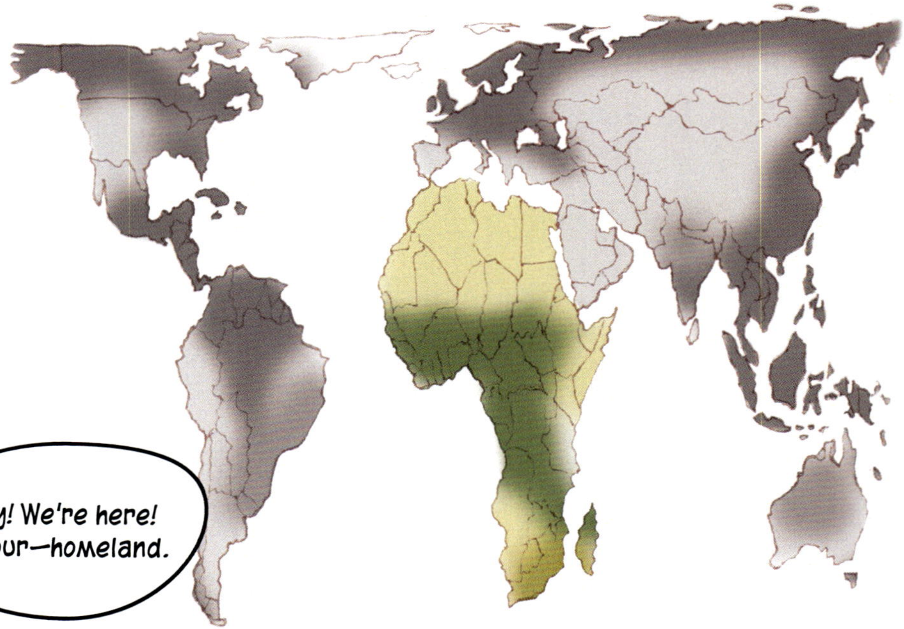

Digging Up the Past

In 1974, scientists dug up the fossilized remains of Dinkinesh in the East African country of Ethiopia. Dinkinesh is a 3.2 million-year-old hominid ancestor. Her name means "you are marvelous," in the Amharic language—one of the main languages in Ethiopia.

Outside Ethiopia, Dinkinesh is mainly known as Lucy—the name given to her by the American **paleoanthropologists** who found her.

Ethiopia isn't the only African country important to the world's early history. Africa is home to some of the most ancient civilizations and kingdoms on Earth.

THE LAND OF KUSH

Kush, later called Nubia, is one of the oldest civilizations in the world. A civilization is an advanced society with government and culture. Researchers date Kush's early beginnings back to approximately 6000 B.C.E.

Kush was located along the Nile River in what is today northern Sudan and southern Egypt. The Nile stretched all the way to the Red Sea. It was also a major transportation route. It brought people together to trade food and goods.

The Nile River also provided the people of Kush with water, fish, and **fertile** soil for farming.

Cradle of Civilization

The early Kushites were nomadic people. They moved with the seasons. Over time, they began permanent settlements called chiefdoms. These settlements came together and were led by a king.

The kingdom of Kush spanned more than 1,400 years (1100 B.C.E.–350 C.E.). The Kushites had their own languages and distinct cultures. They also had their own system of writing.

POWERFUL MALI

The Mali **empire** (1235–1670 C.E.) was one of the largest and most powerful empires in West Africa. It was a multi-**ethnic** center of trade and learning for over 400 years. Mali was ruled by kings called Mansas. A powerful trained army supported the Mansa.

Malian society was divided into different social groups in which people had specific roles and responsibilities. Groups including tradespeople, farmers, miners, merchants, and scholars all helped the kingdom grow and succeed. Blacksmiths, for example, used iron to make utensils, tools, and weapons. Farmers built irrigation systems that brought water to farmland. They grew diverse crops such as kola nuts, peanuts, yams, cotton, and grains. Miners dug gold and salt, which were traded to grow Mali's wealth.

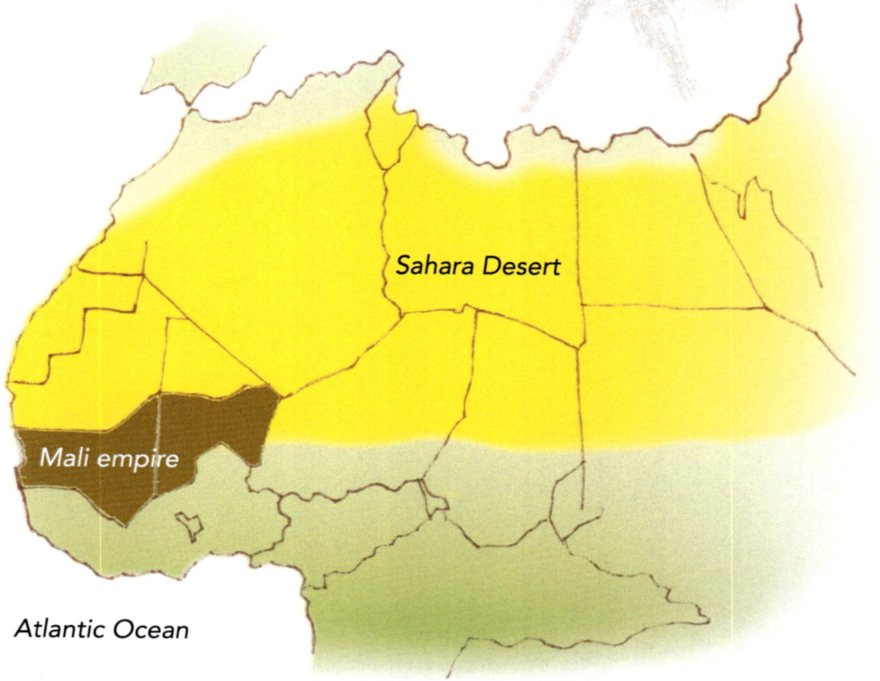

At its peak, the Mali empire stretched from the Sahara Desert in the north to the Atlantic coast in the east.

The Mali empire was at a crossroads of many trade routes. Merchants bought and sold goods from all over the continent.

TRANS-SAHARAN TRADE

The Trans-Saharan trade route was one of the world's oldest and most successful trade routes. At its peak, from the 700s to 1700s C.E., goods were transported across the Sahara Desert by groups of thousands of camels. But the trade route spread more than goods. Rich artistic and storytelling communities flourished in the major trade centers along the route.

Artists created sculptures, pottery, and other art. Dancers and musicians performed. **Griots**, or djelis, told stories, recited poems, and sang songs reflecting history and culture. A new religion also spread. As far back as the 600s C.E., Muslim traders from the Arabian Peninsula and North Africa spread Islam throughout the Mali empire. Over time, Islam became the main religion. Malians read and wrote in Arabic.

One of the world's most ancient centers of learning, the University of Sankore, was built in Timbuktu, in the Mali empire. Scholars there wrote thousands of books on subjects such as medicine, astronomy, and religion.

Sculptors made clay soldiers and archers. These figures showed the military skills of the Malian army.

Cultural Practices

African societies have long histories of diverse social and cultural practices. These are the traditions and customs of social and ethnic groups that express who they are.

Cultural practices include religious and spiritual rituals and ceremonies. Language is also a cultural practice. Some practices are everyday activities. They include what people eat and how they dress themselves.

Cultural practices also include personal grooming, such as how people care for their hair and skin. The stories people tell and the songs they sing are cultural practices, too, because they reflect their lives and histories. Even styles of music and instruments used are culturally created.

Learn about it

Eid al-Fitr is a three-day religious holiday celebrated by Muslims worldwide. It celebrates the end of Ramadan, a month of **fasting** and reflection. Ramadan observes when the Muslim holy book, the Quran, was revealed. During Ramadan, Muslims fast from dawn to sunset. After sunset, they pray together and break the fast with a meal. Eid is a time of joy where Muslims celebrate with family.

"Wise Aleemah." Yup, sounds about right!
It would be cool to learn more about your culture's naming traditions, Kobe.
Kobe, you mentioned the naming ceremony that your parents held for you. I can see how naming traditions are cultural practices that connect people with their heritage. I love the Arabic meaning of my name. "Wise."

NAMING TRADITIONS

In West African cultures, parents traditionally give newborn babies special names based on the day of the week they were born. Day names show a respect for cultural traditions and a connection to ancestors.

Different West African ethnic groups in countries such as Ghana, Nigeria, Benin, Togo, Burkina Faso, and Ivory Coast have different words and meanings for day names. Among the Akan people of Ghana, the name Kobe means "born on Tuesday."

Learn about it

The Akan are the largest ethnic group in Ghana, with many different subgroups. Their naming traditions have lasted centuries. Akan day names can have various spellings and ethnic or regional differences. The chart below shows some examples.

Day of the Week	Boy	Girl
Sunday	Quashee	Quasheba
Monday	Cudjo	Juba
Tuesday	Kobe	Abeni
Wednesday	Quako	Akua
Thursday	Yaw	Aba
Friday	Kofi	Phibba
Saturday	Kwame	Quamina

Oral Traditions

African cultures have strong oral traditions. Storytelling passes messages from one generation to the next. The messages can take the form of songs, poems, sayings, folktales, and **fables**.

In the Mali empire, djelis, or griots, memorized these messages. Djelis trained from an early age. They learned instruments and melodies. They also memorized historical details and kept track of births, deaths, and marriages. They knew histories of families and communities.

Griots preserved, or protected, the stories that would otherwise have been lost. These oral traditions continue to this day.

Some modern West African musicians come from traditional griot families. They connect to the past through music.
Woah... no wonder djelis trained for years. I can barely memorize equations in math class. So cool that griots are the reason so many oral histories survived...I wonder if any of the stories we know today came from griots?
I know one! My gran used to tell me the story of the lion king. It was my favorite thing to hear at bedtime. Not the story in the movie, though. The REAL lion king.

THE LION

The legendary story of the lion king is based on Sundiata Keita, the founder of the Mali empire. Known as the lion prince, he was part of the royal family of the Malinke kingdom.

Sundiata was born after his father, King Naré Maghann Konaté, married Sogolon Kédjou to fulfill a **prophecy** that told him she would give birth to a wise and powerful king. Sundiata was born with a disability that made him unable to walk. He was mocked for this, but Sundiata refused to give in and learned to walk.

When the king died, Sundiata's half-brother, Dankaran Touman, took over. The new king and his mother were cruel to Sundiata and Sogolon. They fled to safety.

Later, Sundiata's people urged him to remember who he was and to return and take over the kingdom. He built an army, worked together with other leaders, and crushed Dankaran Touman. Sundiata called himself Mansa, which means emperor in the Mandinka language. He built one the most powerful empires in the world.

Sounds of the Ancestors

Music has always been a means of communication in African cultures. In the past, talking drums were used for telegraphy, or forms of long-distance communication. Drums were also used for religious and ceremonial purposes, as well as for entertainment.

Some of the world's most well-known instruments came from Africa. The *akonting* is a West African **predecessor** of today's banjo. The *koliko*, *lawa*, and *wase* are West African instruments also similar to the banjo. The *ngoni* and the *xalam* are guitar-like instruments much like the akonting. When their strings are plucked, they make a deep, **resonating** sound.

Djembe drums, made of wood and animal skin, are West African drums played with the hands.

The ngoni (middle) and xalam (bottom) are made from a thin, hollow piece of wood with leather stretched over it.

Enslaved Africans who were stolen, taken far away, and enslaved, never left their culture behind. They made their musical traditions anew in Europe, the Caribbean, and the Americas—passing the rhythms down through the generations. Almost all popular and folk music in the Americas owes much to this history.

The akonting is a long stick with strings attached to a **gourd** body covered in animal skin.

It makes sense that the banjo is an American instrument with roots in Africa. Our people—our ancestors—they brought these songs and skills and knowledge with them when they were stolen from Africa.
Exactly! My family were never enslaved in North America, but in their home village, they have stories about the people who were taken. Those stories were never lost. They were kept by the griots. They sing us our histories...

My gramps took me to the library downtown and they had a griot guest night. She told a story about the pain felt by families in Africa when people were taken and enslaved. She played a xalam, sang, and we answered back. Gramps said it was pretty powerful stuff.
That's a really cool connection. These stories are important in telling us who we are. We were sent here by history! Like, who knew the roots of the banjo came from Africa?
Our people knew. They always knew...

The Transatlantic Slave Trade

African kingdoms established trade with many other empires. Then, beginning in the 1400s, European empires took over territory in North and South America. They built **colonies** and settled Europeans there. The **settlers** grew crops on large farms called plantations.

These plantations needed workers, and settlers found they could make more money if they did not pay for labor. At first, they enslaved the **Indigenous** populations. Then, they turned their interest to Africa. These European empires started the largest global trade of enslaved people in history.

For 400 years, enormous money was made through the trade in enslaved humans and their labor.

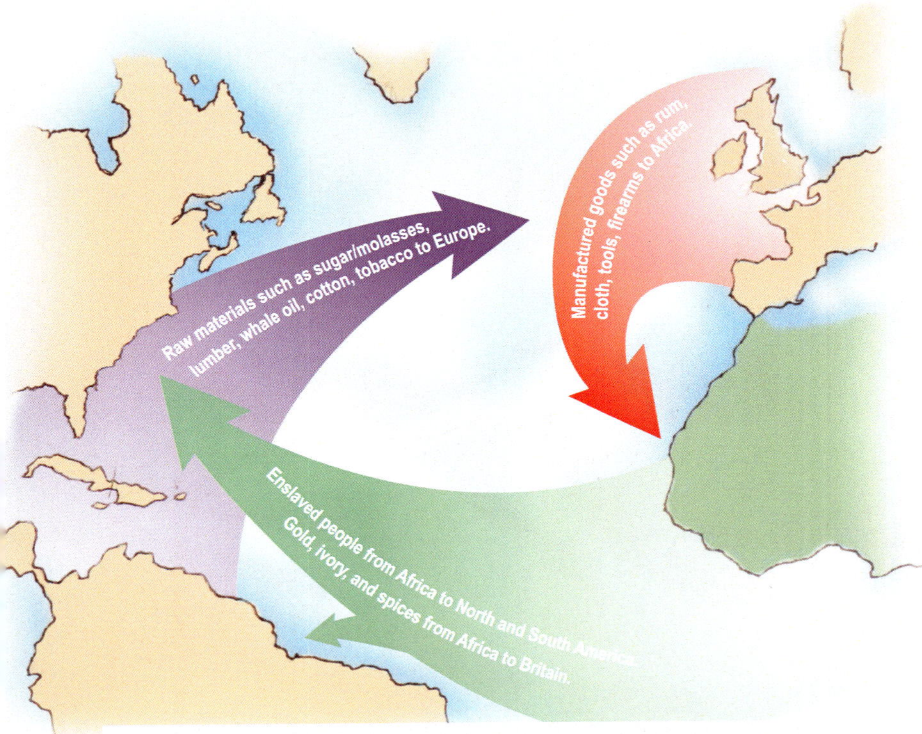

The Portuguese, Spanish, Dutch, French, Danish, and British empires all enslaved African peoples and transported them to their colonies in North and South America.

Triangular Trade

European empires built bases called outposts along the western coast of Africa to expand what is known as triangular trade.

First, ships left European ports with goods such as tools, guns, and alcohol, destined for the west coast of Africa. These goods were exchanged for captured African people taken by African traders.

On the second part of this trading system, the captives were put on slave ships and taken to colonies in the Americas. There, they were sold and enslaved.

The third and final part of the triangle was the return of goods from the Americas to Europe. These goods were produced with the labor of enslaved people.

THE HOUSE OF SLAVES

"Slave castles" were forts or trading posts that were used as holding centers for captive Africans before they were shipped to the Americas. Dozens of these were built along the coast of West Africa. The House of Slaves is a slave castle on Gorée Island, off the coast of Senegal, northeast of Ghana.

Captives were held in the dungeons on the lower floor. Conditions there were horrible, and many captives died before reaching the ships. An estimated 100 to 300 African people were exported from this port each year. Larger forts in what is now Ghana held up to 1,500 captives at a time.

Many slave castles had a "Door of No Return." These were outside doors that captives walked through to board the ships that took them away from Africa.

Today, the island of Gorée is a **UNESCO World Heritage Site**. The homes of traders and the House of Slaves have been preserved as a memorial so people would never forget.

THE MIDDLE PASSAGE

The Middle Passage was the journey from the coast of West Africa to the Americas—or the middle part of the three-part Transatlantic Slave Trade. The Middle Passage took about six weeks. The captives were held in chains and crowded to the point of suffocation.

It is estimated that more than 12.5 million African people were transported across the Atlantic Ocean between 1525 and 1867. Of those, 10.7 million survived the trip. The Transatlantic Slave Trade was a large contributor to the African diaspora. This term refers to the spreading of African people around the world.

Twelve and a half million people! And almost eleven million survivors...my ancestors. Without them, we wouldn't be here.
Yes! They survived all of that. And that's not all they did...

African Resistance

African people did not willingly submit to enslavement. Captives resisted from the time of their capture in Africa, through their journeys to the slave castles, and on the ships that took them to the Americas. To resist is to refuse to accept something, or to fight back against it. There are many examples of captives resisting during the Middle Passage. They organized uprisings on the ships that were transporting them to America. Though most were unsuccessful, some resulted in freedom. These brave actions also drew attention to the cruelties of the Transatlantic Slave Trade.

In 1526, the ruler of the Kingdom of Kongo, Nzinga Mbemba, wrote to the king of Portugal to demand an end to the slave trade that was stealing so many of his people.

Queen Nzinga of Ndongo, or present-day Angola, led a decades-long fight against Portuguese **colonizers** and **slave raiders** in the 1600s.

Agadja Trudo, the king of Dahomey in West Africa (1718–1740), tried to control his territory and the European slave trade within it. At one point he banned it altogether, but was forced to give in.

The Struggle Continues

African resistance continued in the foreign lands to which captives were sent. In North America alone, there were more than 250 recorded uprisings of enslaved people from the 1500s until the mid-1800s. Escaping was another way to resist. Some estimates say that around 100,000 enslaved people in North America escaped to freedom on the Underground Railroad. This was a network of routes and safe houses that aided escaped enslaved people from the late 1700s to the mid-1800s. Enslaved people also resisted through small, everyday actions.

Secretly learning to read and write was an act of resistance taken by some enslaved people.

Learn about it

Enslaved people resisted enslavement in different ways—big and small. Some would take leave without permission for short periods of time. Other forms of personal rebellion included pretending to be ill, working slowly, and breaking or purposely misplacing tools. These small acts came with the risk of punishment—a chance many were willing to take to reclaim some of their personal freedom.

BANNING THE TRADE IN HUMANS

The Atlantic slave trade was banned by Denmark in 1803, by Britain in 1807, and by the United States in 1808. Brazil became the last nation to ban the Atlantic slave trade in 1831. However, illegal trade by merchants in different countries and empires continued throughout the 1800s.

The trade in humans may have been banned, but slavery continued in many areas of the world. It ended in 1834 in the British Empire and colonies of North America. In 1865, the Thirteenth Amendment to the Constitution outlawed slavery in the United States.

March 25 marks the International Day of Remembrance of the Victims of Slavery and the Transatlantic Slave Trade. The day remembers those who were victims of enslavement and raises awareness about the **discrimination** and **racism** faced today because of this history.

Wow, everyone was wrapped up in this trade cycle. How can people treat others this way? It's evil.
Right? I mean 400 years of brutality and has anybody apologized? They passed laws making the Atlantic slave TRADE illegal but still enslaved people!?
I think it's fire that captive and enslaved Africans fought for their freedom...even if it meant death. All kinds of people resisted. I don't think slavery would have ended without that.
Yeah, can I get a "sorry" people? The number of Africans taken is equal to today's populations of Japan and Ethiopia.
I'm glad I was able to learn about this history. It's helping me to understand why Black people back home have said the brutality our people have faced has been happening for a long time.

THE AFRICAN DIASPORA

The Transatlantic Slave Trade was a mass forced removal of African people from their homelands in Africa. It dispersed, or spread, people from many different African kingdoms, empires, and ethnic groups throughout the world. Most were sent to the Americas and the Caribbean.

This dispersal is called the African diaspora. Over time, during and after the end of slavery, people of African descent moved to different countries. Wherever they went, African descendants put down new roots.

Culturally Diverse

The people of the African diaspora are shaped by these different roots and their connection to the history of Africa and its cultural diversity. They have maintained many African traditions. They have also created new ones in their efforts to survive and embrace their identities. Part of the shared experiences of the African diaspora is facing racial discrimination and fighting for **racial justice**.

The Black Lives Matter movement is part of a long tradition of Black social movements. Activism is a way that people of the African diaspora have continued to resist against **oppression** and injustice.

Staying Connected

The history of the continent of Africa is long and deep. Over thousands of years, there were many societies and kingdoms that thrived. Today, there are 54 countries in Africa. It is the second largest continent and has the second highest population. More than 2,000 languages are spoken.

People of African descent spread across the world, through force and by choice. They brought with them their cultural practices, their foods, their ideas, and beliefs that enriched their new societies and communities. African people in the Americas stayed connected to their African roots and created new cultural practices.

Learn about it

Ghana launched a "Year of Return" in 2019 to recognize the 400th anniversary of the first known landing of enslaved African people in Jamestown, Virginia. The Year of Return encouraged the African diaspora to seek out their roots in Ghana and throughout Africa. Since then, more diasporic visitors have come every year.

KOBE
Sooo, our investigation of the meaning of Kobe's name brought us through time and space. I know about my own family's cultural traditions, but I didn't know there was so much overlap in the diaspora. I liked learning about griots. Oral traditions are a part of my culture too.

Before this, the only ancient African empire I knew about was Egypt. Now I know there were so many kingdoms and empires and societies that I want to learn more about. Africa isn't just my ancestors' homeland. It's the place where all human life began. That's so wild!
Fam, I feel like we just got started on our West African diaspora trip. We can just keep going back and digging into the past. Now that I know a little bit, I want to explore more...
No cap! For me, it's the resistance idea, you know? My auntie always says "wi likkle but wi tallawah!" Jamaica is a small country, but don't underestimate us. I guess we all inherited our spirit from our African ancestors...Being part of the African diaspora makes us who we are.

GLOSSARY

ancestors People from whom someone is descended

colonies Areas under the rule of another country

colonizers Countries that send settlers to a place to control it

discrimination Unjust treatment of people, often based on race, gender, age, or ability

empire A group of territories ruled over by a single authority

enslaved Forced into slavery; people without rights or choice who are forced to work without pay

ethnic Relating to groups of people who share a cultural background or descent

fables Stories that pass on morals, or lessons

fasting Abstaining or not eating or drinking something

fertile Land that can grow plants

gourd Dried and hollowed skin of a large fruit

griots West African musicians, poets, storytellers, actors, and historians who share oral histories

Indigenous The original inhabitants of a place

oppression Unjust or cruel treatment or control of a person or group

paleoanthropologists Scientists who study paleontology, or the study of fossils, and anthropology, or the study of human societies

predecessor Something or someone that has been followed or replaced by another

projection An image that is presented on a surface

prophecy A message that predicts the future

racial justice The systematic fair treatment of people from all races that results in equality

racism The beliefs, actions, and systems of power rooted in the idea that a person's race determines their traits, and that one race is superior

resonating A deep and full sound that echoes

settlers People who move to live in a new country or area

slave raiders People who captured others for enslavement

UNESCO World Heritage Site A protected landmark or area singled out as being significant by the United Nations Educational, Scientific, and Cultural Organization

LEARNING MORE

Want to learn more about the African diaspora and African history and culture? Listed below are some books and websites to help you get started.

You can also search online using keywords such as ancient Africa or the Transatlantic Slave Trade. Check your school or public library and search for Black history museums. Read sources from different places to get a fuller picture of the diaspora.

Books

Feelings, Tom. *The Middle Passage*. Penguin Young Readers Group, 2018.

Henry, Natasha. *African Diaspora*. Rubicon Publishing, 2015.

Medieval Africa for Kids. Captivating History, 2023.

Websites

www.slavevoyages.org
Learn more about the history, people, and events of the Transatlantic Slave Trade.

www.blackpeopleshistory.ca

The Black People's History of Canada website offers resources for students and educators to learn and teach about African Canadian history.

www.thegriotmuseum.com

The Griot Museum of Black History in St. Louis preserves Black history and shares the stories of the African diaspora.

www.nmaam.org

The National Museum of African American Music celebrates music created or influenced by African Americans.

Consider This

Traditions such as African day names can teach us a lot about culture. What traditions represent your culture?

How did the Transatlantic Slave Trade result in the African diaspora? Why is it important to know about this history? What steps will you take to learn more?

When Kobe's family first moved from Ghana, they laid down roots in their new community by finding African food stores and restaurants, and an African church. What people, places, or events make up your roots in your community? How do they relate to your family's history?

INDEX

About the Author

Dr. Natasha Henry-Dixon is an assistant professor of African Canadian History at York University. Her multifaceted work reflects her unwavering commitment to researching, preserving, and sharing the histories of Black Canadians.

About the Developer

Alexis Dawson is a community builder, anti-racism trainer, and mother of two. Alexis is a dedicated public education advocate who has served as a trustee on the Toronto District School Board.

About the Illustrator

At the age of nine, Adrian Hayles discovered the expressive power of the visual arts. He later studied illustration and design and began blurring the lines between graffiti and ultra-realism. Founder and director of Toronto's Worth Gallery, Adrian's work can be seen in magazines, video games, animated television shows, and in the 22-storey-high Yonge Love Murals.